This Journal Belongs To

"Life is either a daring
adventure or nothing at all."

~ Helen Keller

A Year in Color

	J	F	M	A	M	J	J	A	S	O	N	D
1												
2												
3												
4												
5												
6												
7												
8												
9												
10												
11												
12												
13												
14												
15												
16												
17												
18												
19												
20												
21												
22												
23												
24												
25												
26												
27												
28												
29												
30												
31												

IRRITATED, FRUSTRATED, OR ANGRY

NERVOUS, STRESSED OR ANXIOUS

ENERGIZED OR EXCITED

CALM OR RELAXED

DEPRESSED, SAD OR EMOTIONAL

ACTIVE, FOCUSED OR MOTIVATED

HAPPY, POSITIVE OR OPTIMISTIC

TIRED, RESTLESS OR UNEASY

One Day at a Time

MONDAY'S **MOOD**

TUESDAY'S **MOOD**

WEDNESDAY'S **MOOD**

Good things take time

THURSDAY'S **MOOD**

One Day at a Time

FRIDAY'S **MOOD**

SATURDAY'S **MOOD**

SUNDAY'S **MOOD**

THOUGHTS & REFLECTIONS ABOUT THE PAST WEEK

Affirmations

DAILY AFFIRMATIONS	IDEAS & PROMPTS

IDEAS & PROMPTS

I'm in charge of how I feel today, and I'm choosing to be happy.

I'm brave enough to climb any mountain.

I have the power to change my story.

I've decided that I'm good enough.

No one can make me feel inferior.

My strength is greater than my struggle.

I'll use my failures as a stepping stone.

It's not their job to like me. It's mine.

Success will be my driving force.

The only person who can defeat me, is me.

I dare to be different.

I do not need other people to be happy.

I deserve love, happiness and success.

I am loved and I am wanted.

I will not apologize for being myself.

Yes,
You Can!

My Mood Today

DRAWING THAT DESCRIBES YOUR **FEELINGS**

It's just a bad day, Not a bad life

Positive Thinking

SELF CARE TO DO LIST:

- ☐
- ☐
- ☐
- ☐
- ☐
- ☐
- ☐
- ☐
- ☐
- ☐
- ☐
- ☐
- ☐
- ☐

PHYSICAL NEEDS

EMOTIONAL NEEDS

HOW I FEEL TODAY

I WANT TO WORK ON...

Self Care Checklist

GOALS	M	T	W	T	F	S	S
Got enough rest	○	○	○	○	○	○	○
Spent time outdoors	○	○	○	○	○	○	○
Drank enough water	○	○	○	○	○	○	○
Spent time doing Something that makes me happy.	○	○	○	○	○	○	○
Went for a walk or exercised.	○	○	○	○	○	○	○
Spent time with family	○	○	○	○	○	○	○
Meditated	○	○	○	○	○	○	○
Connected with friends	○	○	○	○	○	○	○
_____	○	○	○	○	○	○	○
_____	○	○	○	○	○	○	○
_____	○	○	○	○	○	○	○

Mood Meter

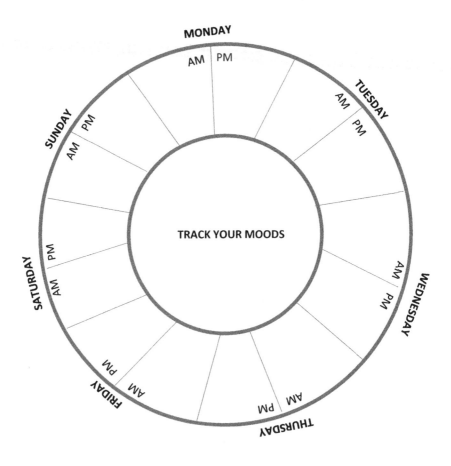

MONDAY

AM | PM

TUESDAY

AM | PM

SUNDAY

PM | AM

WEDNESDAY

AM | PM

TRACK YOUR MOODS

SATURDAY

PM | AM

FRIDAY

PM | AM

THURSDAY

PM | AM

COLOR SCALE

Self Care Log

HOW I CAN **MINIMIZE THE NEGATIVITY** IN MY LIFE

POSITIVE STEPS I CAN TAKE TO BE HAPPY

IT ALWAYS SEEMS Impossible UNTIL IT'S DONE

Self Reflection

SELF REFFLECTION: WHAT MAKES YOU HAPPY?

Each failure brings you one step closer to Success

AFFIRMATION:

Grateful Thoughts

THIS WEEK I AM GRATEFUL FOR

I AM BLESSED TO HAVE THESE PEOPLE IN MY LIFE

5 REASONS TO BE THANKFUL

1
2
3
4
5

Mood Tracker

CREATE A SKETCH THAT REPRESENTS YOUR MOOD

You become what you believe

REFLECTIONS:

Me Time

Write down the things that make you happy. Then, check the box every
day that you spend time with that activity.

Do what makes you Happy

Self Care

DAILY INSPIRATION

WATER INTAKE:

FITNESS GOALS

_____
_____
_____

One day at a time...

THANKFUL FOR

DAILY MEALS

BREAKFAST:

_____
_____
_____

LUNCH:

_____
_____
_____

DINNER:

_____
_____
_____

SNACKS:

_____
_____
_____
_____

Personal Goals

MY SELF GOALS FOR THIS YEAR:

2 THINGS I CAN CHANGE TO MEET MY GOALS:

MY GREATEST OBSTACLE GOING FORWARD:

Good things take time

Mental Health Monitor

DAILY	WEEKLY

PERSONAL REFLECTIONS

Self Care Goals

TIME FRAME	MY GOALS	STEPS I'LL TAKE

be wild ～ be true ～ be happy

Positive Thinking

POSITIVE THOUGHTS:
WRITE DOWN YOUR FAVORITE INSPIRATIONAL PHRASE

Do what makes you Happy

AFFIRMATION:

Self Care Techniques

MIND

BODY

	DATE:

One Day at a Time

MONDAY'S **MOOD**

TUESDAY'S **MOOD**

WEDNESDAY'S **MOOD**

Good things take time

THURSDAY'S **MOOD**

One Day at a Time

FRIDAY'S **MOOD**

SATURDAY'S **MOOD**

SUNDAY'S **MOOD**

THOUGHTS & REFLECTIONS ABOUT THE PAST WEEK

Affirmations

DAILY AFFIRMATIONS

IDEAS & PROMPTS

I'm in charge of how I feel today, and I'm choosing to be happy.

I'm brave enough to climb any mountain.

I have the power to change my story.

I've decided that I'm good enough.

No one can make me feel inferior.

My strength is greater than my struggle.

I'll use my failures as a stepping stone.

It's not their job to like me. It's mine.

Success will be my driving force.

The only person who can defeat me, is me.

I dare to be different.

I do not need other people to be happy.

I deserve love, happiness and success.

I am loved and I am wanted.

I will not apologize for being myself.

Yes, You Can!

My Mood Today

DRAWING THAT DESCRIBES YOUR **FEELINGS**

It's just
a bad day,
Not
a bad life

Positive Thinking

SELF CARE TO DO LIST:

- [ ] _____
- [ ] _____
- [ ] _____
- [ ] _____
- [ ] _____
- [ ] _____
- [ ] _____
- [ ] _____
- [ ] _____
- [ ] _____
- [ ] _____
- [ ] _____
- [ ] _____
- [ ] _____

PHYSICAL NEEDS

EMOTIONAL NEEDS

HOW I FEEL TODAY

I WANT TO WORK ON...

Self Care Checklist

GOALS	M	T	W	T	F	S	S
Got enough rest	○	○	○	○	○	○	○
Spent time outdoors	○	○	○	○	○	○	○
Drank enough water	○	○	○	○	○	○	○
Spent time doing Something that makes me happy.	○	○	○	○	○	○	○
Went for a walk or exercised.	○	○	○	○	○	○	○
Spent time with family	○	○	○	○	○	○	○
Meditated	○	○	○	○	○	○	○
Connected with friends	○	○	○	○	○	○	○
_____	○	○	○	○	○	○	○
_____	○	○	○	○	○	○	○
_____	○	○	○	○	○	○	○

Mood Meter

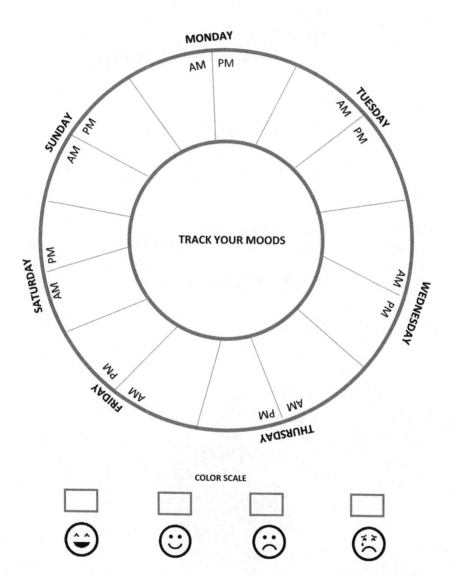

MONDAY

TUESDAY

SUNDAY

SATURDAY

WEDNESDAY

FRIDAY

THURSDAY

TRACK YOUR MOODS

COLOR SCALE

Self Care Log

HOW I CAN **MINIMIZE THE NEGATIVITY** IN MY LIFE

POSITIVE STEPS I CAN TAKE TO BE HAPPY

Self Reflection

SELF REFFLECTION: WHAT MAKES YOU HAPPY?

Each failure brings you one step closer to success

AFFIRMATION:

Grateful Thoughts

THIS WEEK I AM GRATEFUL FOR

I AM BLESSED TO HAVE THESE PEOPLE IN MY LIFE

5 REASONS TO BE THANKFUL

1

2

3

4

5

Mood Tracker

CREATE A SKETCH THAT REPRESENTS YOUR **MOOD**

You become what you believe

REFLECTIONS:

Me Time

Write down the things that make you happy. Then, check the box every day that you spend time with that activity.

Do what makes you Happy

Self Care

DAILY INSPIRATION

WATER INTAKE:

FITNESS GOALS

One day at a time...

THANKFUL FOR

DAILY MEALS

BREAKFAST:

LUNCH:

DINNER:

SNACKS:

Personal Goals

MY SELF GOALS FOR THIS YEAR:

2 THINGS I CAN CHANGE TO MEET MY GOALS:

MY GREATEST OBSTACLE GOING FORWARD:

Good things take time

Mental Health Monitor

DAILY

_____
_____
_____
_____
_____
_____
_____
_____
_____
_____
_____
_____
_____
_____
_____

WEEKLY

_____
_____
_____
_____
_____
_____
_____
_____
_____
_____
_____
_____
_____

PERSONAL REFLECTIONS

Self Care Goals

TIME FRAME	MY GOALS	STEPS I'LL TAKE

be wild ~ be true ~ be happy

Positive Thinking

POSITIVE THOUGHTS:
WRITE DOWN YOUR FAVORITE INSPIRATIONAL PHRASE

Do what makes you **Happy**

AFFIRMATION:

Self Care Techniques

MIND   **BODY**

DATE:

One Day at a Time

MONDAY'S **MOOD**

TUESDAY'S **MOOD**

WEDNESDAY'S **MOOD**

Good things take time

THURSDAY'S **MOOD**

One Day at a Time

FRIDAY'S **MOOD**

SATURDAY'S **MOOD**

SUNDAY'S **MOOD**

THOUGHTS & REFLECTIONS ABOUT THE PAST WEEK

Affirmations

DAILY AFFIRMATIONS	IDEAS & PROMPTS
	I'm in charge of how I feel today, and I'm choosing to be happy.
	I'm brave enough to climb any mountain.
	I have the power to change my story.
	I've decided that I'm good enough.
	No one can make me feel inferior.
	My strength is greater than my struggle.
	I'll use my failures as a stepping stone.
	It's not their job to like me. It's mine.
	Success will be my driving force.
	The only person who can defeat me, is me.
	I dare to be different.
	I do not need other people to be happy.
	I deserve love, happiness and success.
	I am loved and I am wanted.
	I will not apologize for being myself.

Yes,
You Can!

My Mood Today

DRAWING THAT DESCRIBES YOUR **FEELINGS**

It's just
a bad day,
Not
a bad life

Positive Thinking

SELF CARE TO DO LIST:

- [ ] _____
- [ ] _____
- [ ] _____
- [ ] _____
- [ ] _____
- [ ] _____
- [ ] _____
- [ ] _____
- [ ] _____
- [ ] _____
- [ ] _____
- [ ] _____
- [ ] _____
- [ ] _____
- [ ] _____

PHYSICAL NEEDS

EMOTIONAL NEEDS

HOW I FEEL TODAY

I WANT TO WORK ON...

Self Care Checklist

GOALS	M	T	W	T	F	S	S
Got enough rest	○	○	○	○	○	○	○
Spent time outdoors	○	○	○	○	○	○	○
Drank enough water	○	○	○	○	○	○	○
Spent time doing Something that makes me happy.	○	○	○	○	○	○	○
Went for a walk or exercised.	○	○	○	○	○	○	○
Spent time with family	○	○	○	○	○	○	○
Meditated	○	○	○	○	○	○	○
Connected with friends	○	○	○	○	○	○	○
_____	○	○	○	○	○	○	○
_____	○	○	○	○	○	○	○
_____	○	○	○	○	○	○	○

Mood Meter

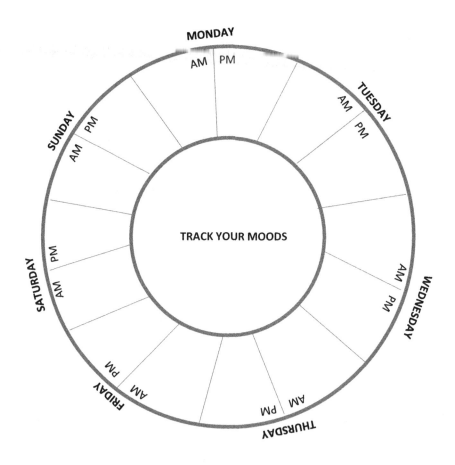

MONDAY

AM | PM

TUESDAY
AM | PM

SUNDAY
AM | PM

SATURDAY
PM | AM

WEDNESDAY
AM | PM

TRACK YOUR MOODS

FRIDAY
PM | AM

THURSDAY
PM | AM

COLOR SCALE

Self Care Log

HOW I CAN **MINIMIZE THE NEGATIVITY** IN MY LIFE

POSITIVE STEPS I CAN TAKE TO BE HAPPY

Self Reflection

SELF REFFLECTION: WHAT MAKES YOU HAPPY?

Each failure brings you one step closer to success

AFFIRMATION:

Grateful Thoughts

THIS WEEK I AM GRATEFUL FOR

I AM BLESSED TO HAVE THESE PEOPLE IN MY LIFE

5 REASONS TO BE THANKFUL

1
2
3
4
5

Mood Tracker

CREATE A SKETCH THAT REPRESENTS YOUR MOOD

You become what you believe

REFLECTIONS:

Me Time

Write down the things that make you happy. Then, check the box every
day that you spend time with that activity.

	☐ ☐ ☐ ☐ ☐ ☐
	☐ ☐ ☐ ☐ ☐ ☐
	☐ ☐ ☐ ☐ ☐ ☐
	☐ ☐ ☐ ☐ ☐ ☐
	☐ ☐ ☐ ☐ ☐ ☐
	☐ ☐ ☐ ☐ ☐ ☐
	☐ ☐ ☐ ☐ ☐ ☐
	☐ ☐ ☐ ☐ ☐ ☐

☆ Do what makes you Happy ☆

Self Care

DAILY **INSPIRATION**

WATER INTAKE:

FITNESS **GOALS**

One day at a time...

THANKFUL **FOR**

DAILY **MEALS**

BREAKFAST:

LUNCH:

DINNER:

SNACKS:

Personal Goals

MY SELF GOALS FOR THIS YEAR:

2 THINGS I CAN CHANGE TO MEET MY GOALS:

MY GREATEST OBSTACLE GOING FORWARD:

Good things take time

Mental Health Monitor

DAILY	WEEKLY

PERSONAL REFLECTIONS

Self Care Goals

TIME FRAME	MY GOALS	STEPS I'LL TAKE

be wild ~ be true ~ be happy

Positive Thinking

POSITIVE THOUGHTS:

WRITE DOWN YOUR FAVORITE INSPIRATIONAL PHRASE

Do what
makes
you
Happy

AFFIRMATION:

Self Care Techniques

MIND

_____
_____
_____
_____
_____
_____
_____
_____
_____
_____
_____
_____
_____
_____

BODY

_____
_____
_____
_____
_____
_____
_____
_____
_____
_____
_____
_____
_____

| | DATE: |

One Day at a Time

MONDAY'S **MOOD**

TUESDAY'S **MOOD**

WEDNESDAY'S **MOOD**

Good things take time

THURSDAY'S **MOOD**

One Day at a Time

FRIDAY'S **MOOD**

SATURDAY'S **MOOD**

SUNDAY'S **MOOD**

THOUGHTS & REFLECTIONS ABOUT THE PAST WEEK

Affirmations

DAILY AFFIRMATIONS

IDEAS & PROMPTS

I'm in charge of how I feel today, and I'm choosing to be happy.

I'm brave enough to climb any mountain.

I have the power to change my story.

I've decided that I'm good enough.

No one can make me feel inferior.

My strength is greater than my struggle.

I'll use my failures as a stepping stone.

It's not their job to like me. It's mine.

Success will be my driving force.

The only person who can defeat me, is me.

I dare to be different.

I do not need other people to be happy.

I deserve love, happiness and success.

I am loved and I am wanted.

I will not apologize for being myself.

Yes, You Can!

My Mood Today

DRAWING THAT DESCRIBES YOUR **FEELINGS**

It's just a bad day, Not a bad life

Positive Thinking

SELF CARE TO DO LIST:

- ☐ _____
- ☐ _____
- ☐ _____
- ☐ _____
- ☐ _____
- ☐ _____
- ☐ _____
- ☐ _____
- ☐ _____
- ☐ _____
- ☐ _____
- ☐ _____
- ☐ _____
- ☐ _____

PHYSICAL NEEDS

EMOTIONAL NEEDS

HOW I FEEL TODAY

I WANT TO WORK ON...

Self Care Checklist

GOALS	M	T	W	T	F	S	S
Got enough rest	◯	◯	◯	◯	◯	◯	◯
Spent time outdoors	◯	◯	◯	◯	◯	◯	◯
Drank enough water	◯	◯	◯	◯	◯	◯	◯
Spent time doing Something that makes me happy.	◯	◯	◯	◯	◯	◯	◯
Went for a walk or exercised.	◯	◯	◯	◯	◯	◯	◯
Spent time with family	◯	◯	◯	◯	◯	◯	◯
Meditated	◯	◯	◯	◯	◯	◯	◯
Connected with friends	◯	◯	◯	◯	◯	◯	◯
_____	◯	◯	◯	◯	◯	◯	◯
_____	◯	◯	◯	◯	◯	◯	◯
_____	◯	◯	◯	◯	◯	◯	◯

Mood Meter

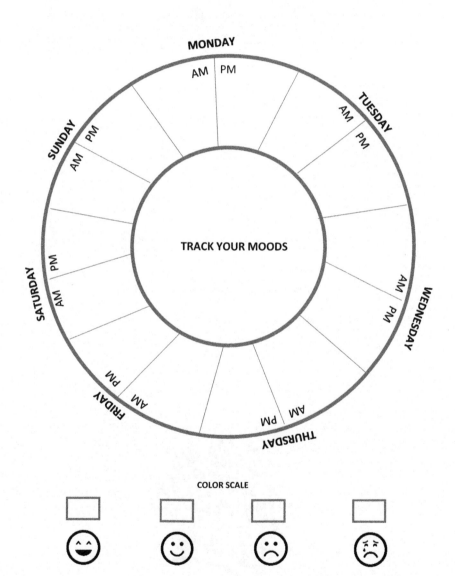

Self Care Log

HOW I CAN **MINIMIZE THE NEGATIVITY** IN MY LIFE

POSITIVE STEPS I CAN TAKE TO BE HAPPY

IT ALWAYS SEEMS Impossible UNTIL IT'S DONE

Self Reflection

SELF REFFLECTION: WHAT MAKES YOU HAPPY?

Each failure brings you one step closer to success

AFFIRMATION:

Grateful Thoughts

THIS WEEK I AM GRATEFUL FOR

I AM BLESSED TO HAVE THESE PEOPLE IN MY LIFE

5 REASONS TO BE THANKFUL

1
2
3
4
5

Mood Tracker

CREATE A SKETCH THAT REPRESENTS YOUR **MOOD**

You
become
what
you
believe

REFLECTIONS:

Me Time

Write down the things that make you happy. Then, check the box every
day that you spend time with that activity.

	☐ ☐ ☐ ☐ ☐ ☐
	☐ ☐ ☐ ☐ ☐ ☐
	☐ ☐ ☐ ☐ ☐ ☐
	☐ ☐ ☐ ☐ ☐ ☐
	☐ ☐ ☐ ☐ ☐ ☐
	☐ ☐ ☐ ☐ ☐ ☐
	☐ ☐ ☐ ☐ ☐ ☐
	☐ ☐ ☐ ☐ ☐ ☐

☆ Do what makes you Happy ☆

Self Care

DAILY **INSPIRATION**

WATER INTAKE:

FITNESS **GOALS**

One day at a time...

THANKFUL **FOR**

DAILY **MEALS**

BREAKFAST:

LUNCH:

DINNER:

SNACKS:

Personal Goals

MY SELF GOALS FOR THIS YEAR:

2 THINGS I CAN CHANGE TO MEET MY GOALS:

MY GREATEST OBSTACLE GOING FORWARD:

Good things take time

Mental Health Monitor

DAILY

_____
_____
_____
_____
_____
_____
_____
_____
_____
_____
_____
_____
_____
_____
_____
_____

WEEKLY

_____
_____
_____
_____
_____
_____
_____
_____
_____
_____
_____
_____
_____
_____

PERSONAL REFLECTIONS

Self Care Goals

TIME FRAME	MY GOALS	STEPS I'LL TAKE

be wild ~ be true ~ be happy

Positive Thinking

POSITIVE THOUGHTS:

WRITE DOWN YOUR FAVORITE INSPIRATIONAL PHRASE

Do what makes you Happy

AFFIRMATION:

Self Care Techniques

MIND

BODY

_____

_____

_____

_____

_____

_____

_____

_____

_____

_____

_____

_____

_____

DATE:

One Day at a Time

MONDAY'S **MOOD**

TUESDAY'S **MOOD**

WEDNESDAY'S **MOOD**

Good things take time

THURSDAY'S **MOOD**

One Day at a Time

FRIDAY'S **MOOD**

SATURDAY'S **MOOD**

SUNDAY'S **MOOD**

THOUGHTS & REFLECTIONS ABOUT THE PAST WEEK

Affirmations

DAILY AFFIRMATIONS

IDEAS & PROMPTS

I'm in charge of how I feel today, and I'm choosing to be happy.

I'm brave enough to climb any mountain.

I have the power to change my story.

I've decided that I'm good enough.

No one can make me feel inferior.

My strength is greater than my struggle.

I'll use my failures as a stepping stone.

It's not their job to like me. It's mine.

Success will be my driving force.

The only person who can defeat me, is me.

I dare to be different.

I do not need other people to be happy.

I deserve love, happiness and success.

I am loved and I am wanted.

I will not apologize for being myself.

Yes, You Can!

My Mood Today

DRAWING THAT DESCRIBES YOUR **FEELINGS**

It's just a bad day, Not a bad life

Positive Thinking

SELF CARE TO DO LIST:

- ☐ _____
- ☐ _____
- ☐ _____
- ☐ _____
- ☐ _____
- ☐ _____
- ☐ _____
- ☐ _____
- ☐ _____
- ☐ _____
- ☐ _____
- ☐ _____
- ☐ _____
- ☐ _____

PHYSICAL NEEDS

EMOTIONAL NEEDS

HOW I FEEL TODAY

I WANT TO WORK ON...

Self Care Checklist

GOALS	M	T	W	T	F	S	S
Got enough rest	○	○	○	○	○	○	○
Spent time outdoors	○	○	○	○	○	○	○
Drank enough water	○	○	○	○	○	○	○
Spent time doing Something that makes me happy.	○	○	○	○	○	○	○
Went for a walk or exercised.	○	○	○	○	○	○	○
Spent time with family	○	○	○	○	○	○	○
Meditated	○	○	○	○	○	○	○
Connected with friends	○	○	○	○	○	○	○
_____	○	○	○	○	○	○	○
_____	○	○	○	○	○	○	○
_____	○	○	○	○	○	○	○

Mood Meter

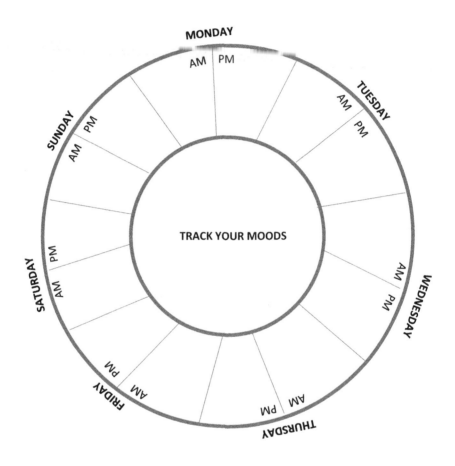

MONDAY
AM | PM

TUESDAY
AM | PM

SUNDAY
PM | AM

WEDNESDAY
AM | PM

TRACK YOUR MOODS

SATURDAY
PM | AM

FRIDAY
PM | AM

THURSDAY
PM | AM

COLOR SCALE

Self Care Log

HOW I CAN **MINIMIZE THE NEGATIVITY** IN MY LIFE

POSITIVE STEPS I CAN TAKE TO BE HAPPY

Self Reflection

SELF REFFLECTION: WHAT MAKES YOU HAPPY?

Each failure brings you one step closer to success

AFFIRMATION:
//

Grateful Thoughts

THIS WEEK I AM GRATEFUL FOR

I AM BLESSED TO HAVE THESE PEOPLE IN MY LIFE

5 REASONS TO BE THANKFUL

1
2
3
4
5

Mood Tracker

CREATE A SKETCH THAT REPRESENTS YOUR **MOOD**

You become what you believe

REFLECTIONS:

Me Time

Write down the things that make you happy. Then, check the box every day that you spend time with that activity.

Do what makes you Happy

Self Care

DAILY **INSPIRATION**

WATER INTAKE:

FITNESS **GOALS**

One day at a time...

THANKFUL **FOR**

DAILY **MEALS**

BREAKFAST:

LUNCH:

DINNER:

SNACKS:

Personal Goals

MY SELF GOALS FOR THIS YEAR:

2 THINGS I CAN CHANGE TO MEET MY GOALS:

MY GREATEST OBSTACLE GOING FORWARD:

Good things take time

Mental Health Monitor

DAILY	WEEKLY

PERSONAL REFLECTIONS

Self Care Goals

TIME FRAME	MY GOALS	STEPS I'LL TAKE

be wild ~ be true ~ be happy

Positive Thinking

POSITIVE THOUGHTS:

WRITE DOWN YOUR FAVORITE INSPIRATIONAL PHRASE

Do what makes you Happy

AFFIRMATION:

Self Care Techniques

MIND

_____

_____

_____

_____

_____

_____

_____

_____

_____

_____

_____

_____

_____

_____

_____

_____

BODY

_____

_____

_____

_____

_____

_____

_____

_____

_____

_____

_____

_____

_____

_____

_____

_____

One Day at a Time

MONDAY'S **MOOD**

TUESDAY'S **MOOD**

WEDNESDAY'S **MOOD**

Good things take time

THURSDAY'S **MOOD**

One Day at a Time

FRIDAY'S **MOOD**

SATURDAY'S **MOOD**

SUNDAY'S **MOOD**

THOUGHTS & REFLECTIONS ABOUT THE PAST WEEK

Affirmations

DAILY AFFIRMATIONS	IDEAS & PROMPTS

IDEAS & PROMPTS

I'm in charge of how I feel today, and I'm choosing to be happy.

I'm brave enough to climb any mountain.

I have the power to change my story.

I've decided that I'm good enough.

No one can make me feel inferior.

My strength is greater than my struggle.

I'll use my failures as a stepping stone.

It's not their job to like me. It's mine.

Success will be my driving force.

The only person who can defeat me, is me.

I dare to be different.

I do not need other people to be happy.

I deserve love, happiness and success.

I am loved and I am wanted.

I will not apologize for being myself.

Yes, You Can!

My Mood Today

It's just a bad day, Not a bad life

Positive Thinking

SELF CARE TO DO LIST:

- [ ] _____
- [ ] _____
- [ ] _____
- [ ] _____
- [ ] _____
- [ ] _____
- [ ] _____
- [ ] _____
- [ ] _____
- [ ] _____
- [ ] _____
- [ ] _____
- [ ] _____
- [ ] _____

PHYSICAL NEEDS

EMOTIONAL NEEDS

HOW I FEEL TODAY

I WANT TO WORK ON...

Self Care Checklist

GOALS	M	T	W	T	F	S	S
Got enough rest	○	○	○	○	○	○	○
Spent time outdoors	○	○	○	○	○	○	○
Drank enough water	○	○	○	○	○	○	○
Spent time doing Something that makes me happy.	○	○	○	○	○	○	○
Went for a walk or exercised.	○	○	○	○	○	○	○
Spent time with family	○	○	○	○	○	○	○
Meditated	○	○	○	○	○	○	○
Connected with friends	○	○	○	○	○	○	○
_____	○	○	○	○	○	○	○
_____	○	○	○	○	○	○	○
_____	○	○	○	○	○	○	○

Mood Meter

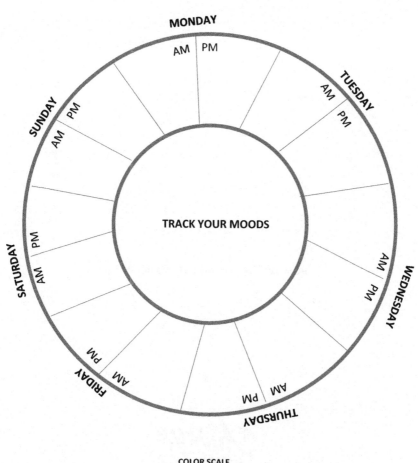

COLOR SCALE

Self Care Log

HOW I CAN **MINIMIZE THE NEGATIVITY** IN MY LIFE

POSITIVE STEPS I CAN TAKE TO BE HAPPY

IT ALWAYS SEEMS Impossible UNTIL IT'S DONE

Self Reflection

SELF REFFLECTION: WHAT MAKES YOU HAPPY?

Each failure brings you one step closer to success

AFFIRMATION:

Grateful Thoughts

THIS WEEK I AM GRATEFUL FOR

I AM BLESSED TO HAVE THESE PEOPLE IN MY LIFE

5 REASONS TO BE THANKFUL

1
2
3
4
5

Mood Tracker

CREATE A SKETCH THAT REPRESENTS YOUR **MOOD**

You become what you believe

REFLECTIONS:

Me Time

Write down the things that make you happy. Then, check the box every
day that you spend time with that activity.

	☐ ☐ ☐ ☐ ☐ ☐ ☐
	☐ ☐ ☐ ☐ ☐ ☐ ☐
	☐ ☐ ☐ ☐ ☐ ☐ ☐
	☐ ☐ ☐ ☐ ☐ ☐ ☐
	☐ ☐ ☐ ☐ ☐ ☐ ☐
	☐ ☐ ☐ ☐ ☐ ☐ ☐
	☐ ☐ ☐ ☐ ☐ ☐ ☐
	☐ ☐ ☐ ☐ ☐ ☐ ☐

☆ Do what makes you Happy ☆

Self Care

DAILY **INSPIRATION**

WATER INTAKE:

FITNESS **GOALS**

_____
_____
_____

One day at a time...

THANKFUL **FOR**

DAILY **MEALS**

BREAKFAST:
_____
_____
_____

LUNCH:
_____
_____

DINNER:
_____
_____

SNACKS:
_____
_____
_____
_____

Personal Goals

MY SELF GOALS FOR THIS YEAR:

2 THINGS I CAN CHANGE TO MEET MY GOALS:

MY GREATEST OBSTACLE GOING FORWARD:

Good things take time

Mental Health Monitor

DAILY

_____
_____
_____
_____
_____
_____
_____
_____
_____
_____
_____
_____
_____
_____

WEEKLY

_____
_____
_____
_____
_____
_____
_____
_____
_____
_____
_____
_____
_____

PERSONAL REFLECTIONS

Self Care Goals

TIME FRAME	MY GOALS	STEPS I'LL TAKE

be wild ~ be true ~ be happy

Positive Thinking

POSITIVE THOUGHTS:
WRITE DOWN YOUR FAVORITE INSPIRATIONAL PHRASE

Do what makes you Happy

AFFIRMATION:

Self Care Techniques

MIND   **BODY**

_____   _____
_____   _____
_____   _____
_____   _____
_____   _____
_____   _____
_____   _____
_____   _____
_____   _____
_____   _____
_____   _____
_____   _____
_____   _____
_____   _____
_____   _____
_____   _____

SOLUTIONS

Made in the USA
Middletown, DE
07 April 2022

63821759R00071